I L♥VE
SHAKESPEARE

First published 2016.

Pitkin Publishing
The History Press
The Mill, Brimscombe Port
Stroud, Gloucestershire GL5 2QG
www.thehistorypress.co.uk

Enquiries and sales: 01453 883300
Email: sales@thehistorypress.co.uk

Text written by Warren King.
The author has asserted their moral rights.

Designed by Chris West.

British Library Cataloguing in Publication Data.
A Catalogue record for this book is available from the British Library.

Publication in this form © Pitkin Publishing 2016.

ISBN 978-1-84165-696-0 1/16

'He was not of an age,
but for all time!'
Ben Jonson

'The remarkable thing about Shakespeare is that he is really very good – in spite of all the people who say he's very good.'
Robert Graves

'If we wish to know the force of human genius, we should read Shakespeare. If we wish to see the insignificance of human learning, we may study his commentators.'
William Hazlitt

Warren King runs the website www.nosweatshakespeare.com with his son; the site contains hundreds of different Shakespeare-related resources, from play texts to study notes.

Contents

CHAPTER
ONE

The Man

1 'Shakespeare' is an ancient surname, seen in Warwickshire since the fourteenth century.

2 Shakespeare's maternal grandfather was Robert Arden. Shakespeare's mother's family had been landowners in the county for more than a century by the time she married Shakespeare's father.

3 Shakespeare's paternal grandfather was probably Richard Shakespeare of Snitterfield, owner of a large farm.

4 Shakespeare's uncle was called Henry ('Hary') Shakspere; he was frequently in debt, and local court records mention him more than once. When he failed to pay up, Shakespeare's father was usually forced to pay instead.

5 Shakespeare was baptised on 26 April 1564. No birthdate is recorded, but as it was customary to baptise a baby on the third day of its life he was most likely born on 23 April 1564.

6 Shakespeare was born and grew up in a house (actually houses, for there were two in the original complex) at Henley Street, Stratford-upon-Avon, Warwickshire. Now known as 'the Birthplace', the house draws more than 2 million tourists every year.

7 Henley Street has existed on Stratford documents from as early as 1369.

8 Shakespeare was living in rented accommodation when he was born: his father only bought the Henley Street properties in 1575, paying Edmund and Emma Hall the sum of £40 for them.

 In his will, Shakespeare offered the Henley Street house to his sister Joan for her lifetime, but left the building to his daughter Susanna.

10 Shakespeare's Birthplace has not always been a house: sold at public auction for £8,000 in 1847, it has been a butcher's shop and a string of pubs, the last one being the Swan & Maidenhead.

11 The records show that 238 Stratford people died of the plague in the year Shakespeare was born: roughly one sixth of the 1,500 or so inhabitants of Stratford-upon-Avon at the time.

12 Shakespeare's father gave eight pence on 20 October 1564 towards the cost of dealing with this outbreak of plague. He also gave twelve pence in the same year 'towardes the releeff of the poure'.

13 William's parents were John and Mary Shakespeare (née Arden). Shakespeare's mother was an heiress, the youngest of eight daughters.

14 Edward Arden, a relative of Shakespeare's mother, was sent to the Tower of London for plotting against Queen Elizabeth I. He was executed: his head may still have been on London Bridge when Shakespeare arrived in the city.

15

John Shakespeare, William's father, moved to Stratford to work as a tradesman in 1551, moving into Henley Street in 1552.

16 Shakespeare's father had many business interests, including as a farmer, glover and tanner. In 1557, he became the official Stratford 'ale-taster', responsible for 'the goodness of bread and ale, or beer'.

17 In 1558, 1559 and 1561, Shakespeare's father was one of Stratford's 'constabulls'. He was later put in charge of setting the fines for crimes that did not already have set penalties.

18 He rose through the Corporation ranks to become high bailiff – i.e chief magistrate – of Stratford by 1568.

19 In 1558, Shakespeare's father and his neighbours were fined four pence for 'not kepynge of their gutters cleane'. Twenty years later, in the 1570s, Shakespeare's father was prosecuted four times for the illegal activities of money-lending and trading in wool.

20 As part of Elizabeth I's Protestant reforms, Shakespeare's father had the Last Judgement scene which covered the walls of the Guildhall chapel painted over, and took the stained glass out of its windows. William may have watched them come down.

21 William's mother Mary gave birth to eight children: Joan, Margaret, William, Gilbert, Joan, Anne, Richard, and Edmund. (The first Joan died very young.)

22 Two more of Shakespeare's siblings died young. When Shakespeare's sister Anne died, at the age of just seven, records show that 'Mr Shaxper' (Shakespeare's father John) paid eight pence for the pall (cloth) that covered her coffin and for the ringing of her funeral bell.

23 The first company of players to perform in Stratford were welcomed by Shakespeare's father (as bailiff) in 1569, when Shakespeare was five.

24 William attended the King's New School, which still stands on the corner of Church Street and Chapel Lane.

25 The Stratford schoolmaster was paid £20 a year to teach Shakespeare. There may have been an assistant master during Shakespeare's time at the school, who would have been paid £10 a year.

26

Although some critics have suggested that Shakespeare was uneducated and couldn't read Latin, during his years at school the curriculum included translating the Geneva Bible into that language.

27 As T. S. Eliot put it, 'We can say of Shakespeare, that never has a man turned so little knowledge to such great account.'

28 It is thought that Shakespeare was taught by Oxford graduates Thomas Jenkins and John Cottom.

29 Shakespeare's grammar school put on classical plays at the end of every term, which some scholars think may have given him the theatre bug.

30 It was the custom of the reigning monarch to go on 'progresses' throughout the land, staying at castles and manor houses across the realm. The Ardens of Park Hall (the family of William Shakespeare's mother) might well have played host to royalty over the years.

31 The 300 carriages that Elizabeth I took with her on progresses included a 'close carriage': a lavatory.

32 Queen Elizabeth I visited Kenilworth Castle, near Stratford, when William Shakespeare was eleven years old.

33 The Shakespeare family, like everyone else in Stratford, would have travelled to Kenilworth to see the Queen and the fireworks, 'sports' (including baiting thirteen bears with large 'ban-dogs') and jousting arranged for her amusement.

34 When Shakespeare was fourteen, his father somehow fell from favour; William and his brothers had to leave school.

35

In 1586, John Shakespeare was stripped of his alderman's gown, because 'he dothe not come to the halles when [he] be warned, nor hathe not done of longe tyme'.

36

Shakespeare's father appears several times in local records for being unable to pay his debts. He may even have gone into hiding from the law: on the 25 September 1592, he appears on a list of Stratford men who refused to go to church 'for feare of processes for debtte'.

37 Shakespeare married Anne Hathaway when he was just eighteen. At twenty-six, she was nearly a decade older than him.

38 Shakespeare's original marriage license was found in a Worcester court in the Victorian era, declaring that 'William Shagspere ... and Anne Hathwey, of Stratford ... maiden, may lawfully solemnise matrimony together'.

39 Anne was already three months pregnant when young William married her; this may have forced the pair to wed.

40 Anne Hathaway's home, known as 'Anne Hathaway's Cottage', is now one of Britain's most visited attractions, and still stands in the village of Shottery, a mile from Stratford.

41 Shakespeare was a teenage father; he was still only nineteen when his first child was born. Her name was Susanna.

42 William Shakespeare later fathered twins: Hamnet (who died when he was only twelve) and Judith.

43

Shakespeare's only son Hamnet is buried with his mother Anne Hathaway in Holy Trinity church, Stratford.

44 William's daughter Judith married a few months before Shakespeare died. She named her first son Shakespeare.

45 It is possible that Shakespeare's father was illiterate; he, as well as Shakespeare's aunt and uncle, all signed their names on some Stratford property documents with a squiggle.

46 It is possible that neither of Shakespeare's daughters could read or write either; his younger daughter Judith, for example, later signed a property deed with a cross. And Shakespeare's wife Anne Hathaway may have been illiterate too.

**47**
Shakespeare left Stratford for London at some point before 1592. The most popular story is that he was fleeing after being convicted of poaching deer from Sir Thomas Lucy at Charlecote, though this is probably not true.

**48**
It is also possible that Shakespeare's father was in prison for debt when the poet left for London: court records show a writ of *habeas corpus* for John on 29 March 1587.

**49**
As W.H. Auden once put it, 'it is great luck that Shakespeare had no money and was forced into drama.'

50 Little information exists about what Shakespeare did in the years from 1585 to 1592, when he moved from Stratford-upon-Avon to London. This era is known as 'the lost years'.

51 It is possible that Shakespeare may have joined a travelling company of players for a time. In 1587, the Queen's Men came to Stratford. Shakespeare may have been one of the performers.

52 Shakespeare may also have been a schoolteacher at some point in his younger years. Other traditions claim that he was a butcher's apprentice before he ran away to London.

THERE IS NO DARKNESS BUT IGNORANCE

53

One tradition has it that Shakespeare's first job in the London theatre was as a 'call-boy', the person who lets the actors know they are about to go on. Another has it that Shakespeare started his career by looking after the horses of people attending the theatre (eventually employing a whole company of stable boys of his own, known as 'Shakespear's boys', to do the job).

54

Other researchers suggest that Shakespeare may have trained as an attorney or as a sailor, because of the legal and maritime terms he uses in his plays.

55

William may have been roped in to edit and revise a text by another writer to make it suitable for staging by the Lord Chamberlain's Men, and in this way got into writing plays for the company.

56

Shakespeare was a professional actor. He took small roles in his own plays, as well as appearing in the work of other playwrights. There are reports that he played the ghost in *Hamlet*, as well as Adam in *As You Like It*.

57

An outbreak of the plague in Europe resulted in all London theatres being closed between 1592 and 1594. As there was no demand for plays during this time, Shakespeare began to write poetry, completing his first batch of sonnets in 1593, aged twenty-nine.

58

The theatres were allowed to open during this time as long as less than thirty people died each week 'within the cittie of London and the liberties thereof'. They did not open often.

59

Shakespeare's poem *Venus and Adonis* was registered on 18 April 1593. It was a bestseller, and during the next few years was reprinted several times.

60

Shakespeare's poetry has since inspired many writers: the poet John Keats, for example, was so influenced by Shakespeare that he kept a bust of the Bard beside him while he wrote, hoping that Shakespeare would spark his creativity.

SHAKESPEARE

THE FIRST FOLIO

Mr WILLIAM
SHAKESPEARES
COMEDIES,
HISTORIES, &
TRAGEDIES.

Publiſhed according
to the True
Originall Copies.

LONDON
1623.

We have but collected
them... and done an
office to the dead:....
without ambition either
of ſelfe-profit, or fame,
onely to keepe the
memory of ſo worthy
a Friend & Fellow aliue,
as was our SHAKESPEARE.

IOHN HEMINGE
HENRY CONDELL.

62

It is not known how long Shakespeare resided in Bishopsgate, but he was definitely living in the parish of St Helen's, as according to the parish records he was assessed on goods valued at £5 and taxed 5 shillings.

61

The first record of William Shakespeare actually living in London has him at Bishopsgate in 1596.

63 Shakespeare's exact Bishopsgate address is unknown, but it is thought to have been in the vicinity of Leadenhall Street and St Mary Avenue.

64 Shakespeare's company the Lord Chamberlain's Men subsequently accepted the patronage of James I and became 'the King's Men'. James was to watch them perform 187 times.

65 James I also gave Shakespeare an official licence to tour: 'Our servants, Lawrence Fletcher, William Shakspeare, Richard Burbage ... freely to use and exercise the art and faculty of plays, comedies, tragedies, histories, interludes, morals, pastorals, stage-plays, &c. &c., as well within their now usual house, called the Globe, within our County of Surrey, as also within any town halls ... or other convenient places within the liberties ... of any other city, university, town, or borough whatever within our realms.'

66 According to contemporary reports, King James himself once wrote William Shakespeare 'an amicable letter', sadly now lost.

67 William Beeston, the son of one of Shakespeare's fellow actors in the Lord Chamberlain's Men, described Shakespeare to John Aubrey (the seventeenth-century version of a gossip columnist) as 'a handsome, well-shaped man: very good company, and of a very ready and pleasant smooth wit'.

68 Shakespeare became a very wealthy man, with a large property portfolio including part-ownership of several theatres.

69 In 1597, when William had become financially successful, he bought 'New Place' in Stratford for the sum of £60. The house stood on the corner of Chapel Street and Chapel Lane.

70

Chapel Lane, where
Shakespeare's house
stood, was called
Dead Lane at the time.

71

New Place was the second
largest house in Stratford.
It was known locally as
'the Great House' when
Shakespeare bought it.
Shakespeare's family lived
there for many years afterwards.

72 Shakespeare's granddaughter eventually sold New Place and all of Shakespeare's land in 1675, raising £1,060.

73 Sadly, however, New Place no longer stands: it was demolished by a subsequent owner, Revd Francis Gastrell, who pulled down Shakespeare's house after falling out with local councillors.

74 Revd Gastrell also chopped down a Mulberry tree planted by Shakespeare: he grew so annoyed with the many sightseers asking to see the tree, in New Place gardens, that he cut it down in 1756.

75 However, fragments of the tree were saved by locals, who kickstarted the tourist souvenir trade by making them into items such as goblets, tooth-pick cases and snuff boxes.

76 In 2013, a single box carved from Shakespeare's Mulberry was sold by Christie's for £13,000. The Birthplace Trust alone has sixty-three items allegedly made from Shakespeare's Mulberry tree.

77 Shakespeare was twelve when the first public playhouse was built. Before the emergence of the public playhouses, plays were performed in private houses and in the courtyards of inns.

78 London's first official playhouse was called 'the Theatre'. It was here that the Lord Chamberlain's company were first based.

79 The world-famous Globe was built with wood stolen from 'the Theatre': in fact, Shakespeare and his friends simply dismantled, transported and rebuilt the entire edifice over the river during the Christmas of 1598.

80

By the turn of the seventeenth century there were at least six further playhouses in London: The Curtain, The Rose, The Swan, The Fortune (pictured), The Red Bull and The Hope.

Upper Stage

Rear Stage

Middle Stage

front Stage

— Yard —

81 At around the same time (1598), Shakespeare's company built a state-of-the-art space at Blackfriars. Before Henry VIII's Dissolution, the Blackfriars' complex had been home to a monastery: the region's name comes from the black robes of the order who lived there.

82 The marriage of Catherine of Aragon and Henry VIII was tried in part of what became Shakespeare's Blackfriars Theatre.

83 Shakespeare was a named partner in the venture, along with James and Richard Burbage. Unfortunately, the neighbours promptly tried to shut the theatre down, 'to the manifest and great injurie of your petitioners, who have no other meanes whereby to maintain their wives and families.'

84 The group was eventually granted the right to keep the theatre – but not to use it! The company considered selling their theatre to the City: Shakespeare demanded £500 for the wardrobe and props. Instead, in time, the popular troupe of child actors who were using the theatre at the time fell out of favour with the Crown, and Shakespeare's company moved back in instead.

85 Children's companies were the vogue in Shakespeare's time. Elizabeth I had four: the Children of St Paul's, the Children of Westminster, the Children of the Chapel and the Children of Windsor.

86 Until the 1970s, the office of *The Times* was next to the Blackfriars Theatre's site.

87 The first hit for Shakespeare's theatre company was not written by Shakespeare, and was not at the Globe: it was Jonson's *Every Man in his Humour* at the Curtain. Shakespeare played Kno'well, one of the main roles.

88 Ben Jonson allegedly got his first break in the theatre because William Shakespeare read and then recommended one of his plays. He later premiered his *Volpone* at the Globe in 1606.

89 Although Jonson commented on Shakespeare's lack of a classical education – mocking his 'small Latin and less Greek' – they were close friends. As well as *Every Man in his Humour*, Shakespeare is known to have performed in Jonson's *Sejenus*. Unfortunately, we don't know which role he took.

90 By 1598 Shakespeare was living somewhere within a minute's walk of the building site that was to become the Globe Theatre. The theatre was to become the company's summer space; in the winter, from 1608, the company would return to their new enclosed complex at Blackfriars.

91 Shakespeare was to become a formidable businessman: as well as earning a fee for each play he wrote, he was also a shareholder in the company and therefore shared in the profits of each play.

92 His new lodging was somewhere in the tiny area known as the Liberty of the Clink, which surrounded the notorious prison of that name. His neighbours near the Clink included Mr Sparrowhauke and Mr Badger.

93 There is a record of a case of tax avoidance against Shakespeare being referred to the Bishop of Winchester in 1598.

94 Shakespeare's pen – and a verse written in his hand – may be buried in the tomb of Edmund Spenser at Westminster Abbey: it is known that all the well-known poets of the day attended Spencer's burial in January 1599, and there threw quills and verses into his grave before it was closed.

95 Westminster Abbey searched for Spenser's grave in 1938. Sadly, however, they could not find the exact site of his grave.

96 As Shakespeare developed as a writer, his techniques and themes developed too. By 1600 Shakespeare had reached maturity as a writer and most of his greatest plays were written on or around that date, including *Hamlet* and *Macbeth*.

97 Shakespeare's father died intestate in September 1601. Bizarrely, however, his will (real or forged) was found hidden in the roof of William's Birthplace in 1770. In it he repented of being 'a most abominable and grievous sinner', and declared himself to be a Catholic.

98 According to Archdeacon Richard Davies of Lichfield, who had known Shakespeare, William Shakespeare was also Catholic. (Though William would have received an Orthodox Protestant education at school.)

99 Queen Elizabeth I watched a play called *Othello* in 1602. 'Burbidges players' were paid £10 for the performance. It was performed again, for James I, at Whitehall in 1604.

100 Shakespeare spent 1603 on an acting tour of the country, and then went home to Stratford, where he worked on classics including *King Lear*: a vicious outbreak of plague had again closed all the London theatres.

101 By 1604 Shakespeare was back in London, living in Silver Street, St Paul's, in an upstairs room in the house of the Mountjoys, a French Huguenot family.

102 He later testified in a bitter and complex court case between his landlord, wigmaker Christopher Mountjoy, and Mountjoy's son-in-law, Stephen Bellott, who was suing Mountjoy concerning the marriage dowry. Shakespeare appeared as a witness in the case.

103 The Mountjoy house was destroyed in the Great Fire and the whole area was flattened during the Blitz of the Second World War.

104 In 1613 Shakespeare bought a house known as The Gatehouse, on the north-eastern corner of the large Blackfriars Theatre's site. He bought the house from Henry Walker for £140 but never lived there. Shakespeare later left The Gatehouse to his daughter Susanna.

105 The Cockpit pub on St Andrew's Hill (near St Paul's), which has been a pub since Shakespeare's day, stands near to where Shakespeare's Gatehouse once stood.

106 Shakespeare's house was destroyed in 1666, during the Great Fire of London.

107

William Shakespeare's youngest brother Edmund was also an actor in London. He died in 1607, at the age of twenty-seven.

108

William paid twenty shillings to have his brother Edmund buried in St Saviour's, Southwark, 'with a forenoone knell of the great bell'. William paid an extra shilling for the ringing of the bell.

109

Shakespeare secured a family crest for his father (making him a gentlemen) from the College of Arms before he died: a yellow spear on a yellow shield, with a falcon on top and the Latin inscription 'Non Sans Droit' ('Not Without Right').

110

Shakespeare's pedigree claims an ancestor who was squire to King Henry VII. This may not have been true, however, as a contemporary writer (1580) wrote that any applicant 'shall for monie have a cote and armes bestowed upon him by the heralds, who ... *doo of custome pretend antiquities and service, and manie gaie things*'.

111

Shakespeare read and wrote French. He wrote an entire scene in French for *Henry V* (Act III, Scene IV).

112

Words invented by Shakespeare include *accommodation, apostrophe, assassination, bump, countless, courtship, generous, gloomy, laughable, lonely* and *suspicious.*

113 Less popular today (but more dramatic) is Shakespeare's word *multitudinous*:'What hands are here? Hah! They pluck out mine eyes. Will all great Neptune's ocean wash this blood clean from my hand? No; this my hand will rather the multitudinous seas incarnadine, making the green one red!'

114 Phrases first used by Shakespeare include *bare-faced, break the ice, catch a cold, disgraceful conduct, eat out of house and home, fair play, foregone conclusion, heart of gold, hot-blooded, one fell swoop,* and *too much of a good thing.*

115 Among the many curse words in Shakespeare's plays are *marry*, a play on the Virgin Mary; *zounds*, a shortening of Christ's wounds; *snails*, Christ's fingernails; and *steeth*, 'Christ's teeth'.

116 Elizabeth I was apparently very fond of swearing – as were her people. English writer Philip Stubbs (or Stubbes) once wrote that the English, 'if they speake but three or four words, yet they must be interlaced with a bloudie oath or two.'

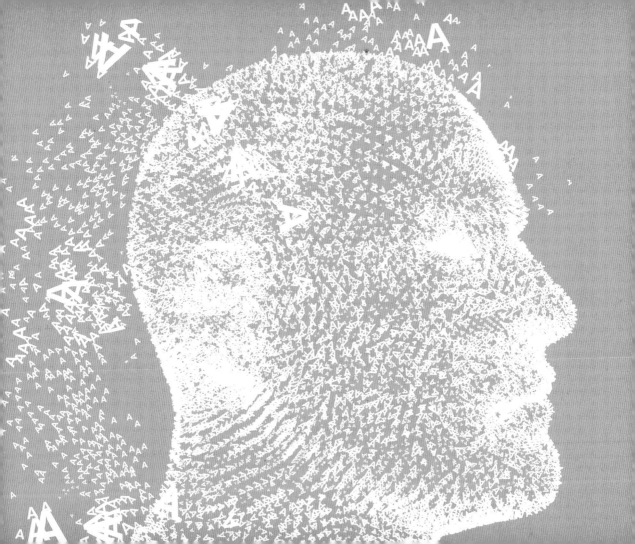

117
In total, Shakespeare has been credited by the *Oxford English Dictionary* with introducing more than 1,000 words to the English language.

118
Estimations of Shakespeare's vocabulary range from 17,000 to 29,000 words. According to Shakespeare professor Louis Marder, 'Shakespeare was so facile in employing words that he was able to use over 7,000 of them – more than occur in the whole King James version of the Bible – only once and never again.'

119
Shakespeare set thirteen of his plays either fully or partly in Italy. However, in spite of so many of his plays being set in European countries, Shakespeare never travelled out of England – or at least, no one has ever been able to produce any evidence of his having done so.

120
The forty-sixth word of Psalm 46 is 'shake' and the forty-sixth word from the end of the same Psalm is 'spear'. Some think this was a hidden birthday message to Shakespeare from its authors, as the King James Bible was published in April 1611, the year of Shakespeare's forty-sixth birthday.

121

During his years of retirement, Shakespeare enjoyed a rich social life, visited by some of the most glittering stars of the age (including men like Ben Jonson and Michael Drayton).

122 According to a manuscript at Dulwich College, Shakespeare's friends called him Will ('Willes newe playe').

123 The tradition is that Shakespeare died on his fifty-second birthday, 23 April 1616.

124 There is only one account of Shakespeare's death and the cause of it. In 1661, many years after Shakespeare's death, John Ward, vicar of Holy Trinity Church in Stratford, noted in his diary: *'Shakespeare, Drayton, and Jonson had a merry meeting, and it seems drank too hard; for Shakespeare died of a fever there contracted.'*

125 Shakespeare was buried in Holy Trinity Church in Stratford-upon-Avon on 25 April 1616.

126 His wife, daughter and son-in-law were later buried nearby.

127 His epitaph contains a warning: *'Blest be the man that spares these stones, And curst be he that moves my bones.'*

128 Perhaps heeding this warning, Shakespeare's remains have never been disturbed.

129

Shakespeare's original grave marker showed him holding a bag of grain. Citizens of Stratford replaced the bag with a quill in 1747.

130

In 1793, Shakespeare's colourful bust was whitewashed. It remained that way until 1851.

131 Shakespeare's will begins, 'In the name of God! amen. I William Shackspeare, of Stratford upon Avon in the countie of Warr. gent. in perfect health and memorie, God be praysed.... commend my soule into the handes of God my creator.' It ends, 'by me, William Shakspeare'.

132 Shakespeare left his clothes to his sister Joan. They became a sort of fancy-dress box, and one of her descendants 'well remembered' dressing up 'in the wearing apparel of our Shakspeare'.

133 The only mention of Shakespeare's wife in his will is: 'I gyve unto my wief my second best bed with the furniture [bedclothes].'

134 Shakespeare has no direct descendants. His four grandchildren (Shakespeare, Elizabeth, Richard and Thomas) all died without heirs.

135

The National Portrait Gallery's first acquisition, in 1856, was the 'Chandos' portrait of Shakespeare (attributed to the artist John Taylor, although some suggest that it was painted by Shakespeare's business partner and leading man Richard Burbage).

136

The Chandos portrait is now considered the only representation of the writer that has any real claim to having been painted from life.

CHAPTER
TWO

The Works

Mr. WILLIAM
SHAKESPEARE
COMEDIES,
HISTORIES, &
TRAGEDIES.
Published according to the True Originall Copies.

LONDON
Printed by Isaac Iaggard and …

 **137** *The Comedy of Errors* is Shakespeare's shortest play, at just 1,770 lines long.

 **138** At 4,042 lines, *Hamlet* is his longest play. Unedited, it takes more than four hours to perform.

 **139** The first play written by William Shakespeare could be any one of eight different choices: the author favours *Henry VI Part I*.

 **140** Shakespeare most probably wrote his last play – a collaboration called *The Two Noble Kinsmen* – in 1613, when he was forty-nine years old.

 **141** Of his characters, Hamlet (1,422 lines) has the most lines, and Falstaff the second most (1,178 lines in total).

142

During his writing life, Shakespeare wrote an average of one and a half plays a year. He wrote or co-wrote thirty-seven plays that we know of (plus *Love's Labour's Won*, which may be a play unknown to us), as well as 154 sonnets and some epic poems too.

143

Researchers claim that Shakespeare may have written as many as twenty further plays, all of which have been lost.

144

However, as Bill Bryson points out, less than 250 play texts still exist from Shakespeare's time, so Shakespeare's work is actually very well represented.

145

On 13 December 1727, theatre impresario Lewis Theobald staged a performance of a play titled *Double Falsehood* at the Drury Lane Theatre. He announced that he had uncovered three prompt books for the play which proved it had been written by William Shakespeare. Theobald's claim was generally dismissed, but modern scholars believe it may really have been based on a lost play, *Cardenio*.

146

Cardenio may have been inspired by an episode in *Don Quixote* involving a lover driven to madness. Weirdly, Cervantes also died on the same day as Shakespeare.

147

Shakespeare did not simply sit down and write a play straight off: he was continuously juggling with several writing projects: his own plays, collaborations with others, revising, editing, and writing sonnets.

148

In Elizabethan theatre circles it was common for writers to collaborate on writing plays. Towards the end of his career Shakespeare worked with other writers: *Timon of Athens* was a collaboration with Thomas Middleton; *Pericles* with George Wilkins; and *The Two Noble Kinsmen* (his last play) with John Fletcher.

149

The British Library has part of the manuscript for the play *Sir Thomas More*. There are notes by six different writers detectable on this manuscript, one of whom is possibly Shakespeare. If true, this is the only surviving example of Shakespeare's writing apart from his signature.

Five genuine Autographs of Shakspeare.

Nº 1

2

3

4

5

Nº is from Shakspeare's Mortgage 1612-13.

150

There are more than eighty contemporary variations in the spelling of Shakespeare's name. He himself spelt his name 'Willm Shaksp,' 'William Shakespe,' 'Wm Shakspe,' 'William Shakspere,' 'Willm Shakspere,' and 'William Shakspeare'.

151

However, there are no records of him ever having spelt it 'William Shakespeare'!

152

Authorship controversies are not a new phenomenon: the first recorded reference to Shakespeare, written by fellow playwright Robert Greene in 1592, was as an 'upstart crow, beautified with our feathers'.

153

However, a powerful argument for Shakespeare being the author of the plays is that the texts are sprinkled with slang words used only by people from Stratford, such as 'ballo', a wooden stick used as a weapon; 'gallow', to frighten; 'geck', an idiot, and 'pash', to hit someone.

154

The most amusing theory, mentioned in Paul Edmondson's *Shakespeare Beyond Doubt*, is that Shakespeare bought other writers' plays and then 'spiced [them up with] with obscenity, blackguardism, and impurities'.

155

Edward de Vere, 17th Earl of Oxford, one of the most popular suggestions for the 'real Shakespeare', first went to university at eight, killed a man at seventeen, was once captured by pirates, banned his wife from speaking to him for five years, impregnated Queen Elizabeth's maid and once accidentally spent more than £3,000 on Fool's Gold.

156 De Vere's other claims to fame include declaring that Queen Elizabeth had the 'worst' singing voice.

157 Sir Francis Bacon, another popular candidate for the 'real' Shakespeare, allegedly died from pneumonia contracted after stuffing a chicken with snow as part of a scientific experiment.

158 James Barrie of *Peter Pan* fame had an amusing retort when asked his opinion on who actually wrote the plays: 'I know not, sir, whether Bacon wrote the works of Shakespeare, but if he did not it seems to me that he missed the opportunity of his life.'

159 Shakespeare never actually published any of his plays. They are known today only because two of his fellow actors – John Hemminges and Henry Condell – recorded and published thirty-six of them seven years after his death as 'the First Folio', which is the most reliable version of his plays.

160 There are only 232 known copies of the First Folio in existence. When published, a copy of the First Folio cost £1; in 2001, a copy sold for £4.3 million.

161 The Royal Library at Windsor has a copy of the Second Folio with Charles I's handwritten notes in it. He wrote *Dum Spiro Spero* in it: whilst I breathe, I hope.

162 The owner of one First Folio, Harry Widener, went down with the *Titanic*.

163 Anne Hathaway outlived Shakespeare by seven years, and died in the same year that the First Folio was published.

164

There are also more than 70 'quarto' editions, published in Shakespeare's lifetime and recording twenty-one of his plays. However, these are less reliable: no one knows where they originated, but most of them appear to have been pirated – i.e written down as a performance was taking place, with all the errors, omissions and additions that entails.

165 The Globe was a round theatre inside, which Shakespeare refers to as 'this wooden O' in the chorus of *Henry V*, but a polygon (with twenty sides) from the outside.

166 The original Globe theatre may have been attached to a tavern.

167 Play performances began at between 2 p.m. and 3 p.m, depending on the month. It meant that a play like *Hamlet* couldn't be performed at the Globe during the autumn or winter, as the light would fail before the end of the play.

168 A flag was flown over the Globe to show a performance was about to begin.

169 Elizabethan playhouses were mainly open, with a stage jutting out into the central arena where most of the audience stood. When Elizabethan audiences arrived at the Globe for a performance they placed a penny in a pottery box at the door. That would be enough for standing tickets.

170 Standing members of the audience were known as groundlings (a kind of fish that stares up from the bottom of rivers with its mouth gaping open). Ben Jonson called the groundlings 'the *understanding* gentlemen of the ground'.

171 To progress to the seats, visitors at the Globe would have to put a penny in another box at the foot of the stairs, and another penny in a third box to advance to the second gallery.

172 The money boxes from all three levels were then taken to a special office at the back – the origin of the term 'box office' – and smashed open. The money was counted and the profits shared among the theatre owners and the players.

173 Galleried seating, beneath a roof, and even private 'rooms' with a key, were available for those who could afford them. Wealthy people could even pay to sit on the stage during performances: *The Gull's Horn-book* of 1609 describes how you could 'laugh aloud in the middle of the saddest scene of the terriblest tragedy' if you wanted the audience to watch you rather than the actors.

174 During play performances, the audience would shout to the actors – and if they were dissatisfied with anything, they would throw things at them. The rich people on the stage would also talk to the actors, commenting on the action.

175

Play texts were usually hastily written for performance on stage, and were disposable. It is mainly for this reason that none of Shakespeare's original manuscripts exist.

176

In some instances, the actors got their lines only once the play was in progress – often in the form of a player acting on the stage as a prompt backstage whispered his lines to him shortly before he was supposed to deliver them.

177 Elizabethan and Jacobean theaters generally used little scenery. Instead, playwrights described the setting within the text of the performance: 'But, look, the morn, in russet mantle clad/Walks o'er the dew of yon high eastward hill.' However, they did use special effects including thunder, lightning (with real bolts), smoke and flames.

178 Large painted pillars supported a canopy over the stage, decorated with the sun, moon and stars. It represented heaven. Actors could be made to fly by lowering them on ropes through trapdoors in the ceiling.

179 A section was curtained off at the back of the stage so characters could hide from the audience's view. The curtains could also part to reveal a new location (a witch's cave, say) – or a body, like Polonius's. Above this ran an upper balcony stage, also curtained, where Juliet could appear as she dreamt of Romeo.

180 The area below the stage represented hell, and actors could be raised up and lowered through trapdoors. Some stage jokes relied on this: the ghost in *Hamlet*, for example, calls out to Hamlet from under the stage, and Hamlet replies to 'this fellow in the cellarage'.

181 Shakespeare is most often referred to as an Elizabethan playwright, but he is in fact more of a Jacobean writer. His later plays show the distinct characteristics of Jacobean drama, including plotting and scheming, sex, and extreme violence.

182 However, Elizabethan audiences loved seeing violence on the stage too, and Shakespeare was an enthusiastic fan of gore. Modern theatre would have difficulty coming up with anything like the horrors of *Titus Andronicus*, for example. Shakespearean stage directions include *enter a messenger with two heads and a hand* and *he plucks out his eyes*.

183 According to Bill Bryson, Shakespeare uses the word 'bloody' 226 times in his works. Neil MacGregor, meanwhile, counts 45 references to torture and torturers.

184 The thirst for gore was so pronounced that Jacobean plays usually ended with a blood-drenched stage. Stage blood was created by using bladders filled with pigs' or sheep's blood.

185 Laurence Fishburne (of *Matrix* trilogy fame), who played Othello in the film of 1995, once said: 'Sex and violence is not that new. I mean, Shakespeare was an actor too. So, he wrote, it seems to me, things that he knew actors would love to play.'

186

It was illegal for women to perform in the theatre in Shakespeare's lifetime, so all the female parts were written for boys. The first woman did not appear on the English stage until the Restoration of Charles II.

187

Elizabethan audiences loved puns and would applaud loudly when they appeared in the plays. Shakespeare accordingly obliged them by including an enormous number in his texts.

188

Elizabethans were prohibited by law from dressing above their rank. Players were the only exception to this rule, and could dress as noblemen on stage but not as they walked about the streets.

189

Often (as one foreign visitor noted in 1599), actors wore the clothes of real English nobility on stage: servants were given their master's old clothes but were not legally allowed to wear them, so they sold them to the theatres instead. King James briefly closed the Globe after the King's Men bought the just-retired Spanish Ambassador's clothes and wore them in a play that satirized his failure to arrange a marriage between the king's son and the Infanta.

190

For the Roman plays, actors wore sheet-like robes.

191 Most of Shakespeare's plays required musicians on the stage. Shakespeare is in fact one of the most successful songwriters in history: his songs are still regularly performed on stages around the world as part of his play performances.

192 Theatre performances usually ended with a dance or a jig (a song-and-dance routine).

193 Will Kempe, the actor who usually played jesters and burlesque characters, was an accomplished dancer and led the jigs that ended each play at the Globe. In 1600, Kempe Morris-danced all the way from London to Norwich.

194 Elizabethan playwrights were well paid. Typically, they would receive between £5 and £10 for a play: the same as a craftsman or shopkeeper would make in a year.

195

However, acting was *not* a highly paid or highly respected profession: actors were regarded as vagrant troublemakers who lived rough and sinful lives.

196 Copyright didn't exist in Shakespeare's time, and as a result there was a thriving trade in copied plays. 'Table-books' were small plates of slate on which you could copy the dialogue down as it was spoken.

197 Policing copyright theft would have been almost impossible anyway, given the enormous number of theatregoers in Shakespeare's time: James Shapiro estimates that 'over a third of London's adult population [in Shakespeare's lifetime] saw a play every month'.

198 Bill Bryson estimates that 50 million people attended London's theatres in just seventy-five years.

199 James I was one of the most passionate proponents of the stage: one account says that he saw five times as many plays as Elizabeth in a single year.

200 The first play watched by King James I when he reached England was performed by Shakespeare's company at Lord Pembroke's house at Wilton.

201

James I gave Shakespeare's company £30 to help keep them going whilst plays were prohibited 'by reason of the greate perill that might growe through the extraordinarie concourse and asseemblie of people to a newe increase of the plague'.

SUPPLEMENT TO THE ILLUSTRATED LONDON NEWS, JUNE 8, 1912.—XV

BY SHAKESPEARE'S COMPANY OF "KING'S SERVANTS": A "COMMAND."

DRAWN BY A. FORESTIER.

WATCHING HIS GREAT-GRAND-UNCLE: KING JAMES I. AT A PERFORMANCE OF "KING HENRY VIII." IN WHITEHALL PALACE.

"Writing in the "Times" not long ago, on the Tercentenary of the production at Company of his Majesty's Players, Mr. Ernest Law said: "At the disposal of the actors and courtliness invented by Inigo Jones for the Royal Masques. . . . Already even in the time of Queen Elizabeth, as well as in the earlier years of James I., before the full

202

In around 1200 AD, Saxo Grammaticus wrote *Gesta Danorum* ('Deeds of the Danes') which chronicled Denmark's Kings and told the story of Amleth: the source of *Hamlet*. It is believed that Shakespeare would have had to work from the original Latin.

203 The first performance of *Hamlet* was by the King's Men at The Globe between 1600 and 1601. One contemporary manuscript records that Shakespeare was paid £5 for the play.

204 The first actor to play Hamlet was Richard Burbage, Shakespeare's friend, fellow actor and business partner, the most famous actor of his generation and for whom Shakespeare wrote most of his tragic roles.

205 Burbage was the first 'method actor', adopting the persona of a character and living it both on the stage and in his daily life.

206 Burbage is buried in St Leonard's Church, Shoreditch. The inscription on his tombstone reads 'Exit Burbage'.

207

The castle, Elsinor, where *Hamlet* is set, actually exists. It is called Kronborg Castle and is in the Danish port of Helsingør. It was built in 1423 by the Danish king Eric of Pomerania.

208

King James I and Anne, Princess of Denmark, married (by proxy) at Elsinor Castle in 1589.

209 More than 200 women have played Hamlet on the professional stage. The first woman to play Hamlet was Sarah Siddons, the toast of Drury Lane, who was famous in her time for her Lady Macbeth. She first played Hamlet in 1776.

210 In 1787 *Hamlet* was performed in the Richmond Theatre. Hamlet was played by an actor named Cubit who had never had a speaking part. He was heckled off the stage by the audience and refused to go back for the next performance. The play was then performed without the presence of the main character.

211 The skull held by actor David Tennant (most famous for playing *Dr Who*) in the RSC's 2008 production of *Hamlet* was real: pianist Andre Tchaikowsky left his skull to the company in his will, 'for use in theatrical performance'.

212

The *Henry IV* character Sir John Falstaff was so popular with audiences (and with Queen Elizabeth I) that Shakespeare transplanted him into a comedy, *The Merry Wives of Windsor*.

213

Falstaff was originally named Sir John Oldcastle, but the Cobham family, descended from the original Oldcastles, protested. William Brooke, 10th Baron Cobham, who was Queen Elizabeth's Lord Chamberlain, must have been insulted by the fat knight's use of his family name.

214 In *Henry IV* Part 1, Falstaff eats a loaf of bread and a capon, washed down with two gallons of sherry – at a cost of more than the weekly earnings of a skilled artisan. Sir Walter Scott, who was in the audience of one such performance, reported that the feast was an improvement on the first night and, indeed, an improvement on the play itself.

215 Catherine the Great of Russia opened her Hermitage Theatre in St Petersburg in 1786. The first production was *What it is to have Linen and Buckbaskets*, her own adaptation of *The Merry Wives of Windsor*. Catherine also translated *Timon of Athens* into Russian.

216 Masques – the combination of drama, song and dance – became popular during the reign of James I. Shakespeare demonstrated his mastery of the masque form with his last solo play, *The Tempest,* which resembles a modern musical.

217 Beethoven's *Piano Sonata No. 17 in D minor* is usually referred to as 'The Tempest' after his friend Anton Schindler claimed that the sonata had been inspired by the play.

218 The Friar's letter in *Romeo and Juliet* – originally known as *The Most Excellent and Lamentable Tragedie of Romeo and Juliet* – is prevented from arriving because the delivery boys have been locked inside a plague house.

219 Charles Dickens' last written words were a quotation from *Romeo and Juliet*: 'These violent delights have violent ends.'

220 In the source material for *Othello*, Desdemona is knocked out with a sandbag and then crushed by a roof which the Moor collapses on top of her.

221 James I enjoyed *The Merchant of Venice* so much that he ordered a second performance less than a week after he'd first seen it, on 10 February 1605.

222 *A Midsummer's Night's Dream* may have been written to celebrate a wedding – though whose, we don't know.

223

According to Eric Rasmussen's *The Shakespeare Thefts*, *Measure for Measure* was ripped out of a Spanish copy of the Second Folio by members of the Spanish Inquisition. The same Inquisitor rated *The Merry Wives of Windsor*, *The Comedy of Errors*, *Much Ado* and *The Merchant of Venice* 'good'.

224 The earliest mention of *Twelfth Night* refers to a performance for the barristers of Middle Temple in February 1602.

225 Malvolio's yellow stockings in *Twelfth Night* were meant to be worn with Puritan black robes; his character may have been inspired by a famous Tudor Puritan and exorcist called John Darrell, who was sent to prison for fraud. The devils' names used by Edgar in *King Lear* (Flibbertigibbet, Smulkin) were first published in a book about that scandal.

226 The geographical setting of *Antony and Cleopatra* is the whole world as it was known in Roman times. The ancient Greek historian and philosopher Plutarch was the main source for Shakespeare's Roman plays. including *Antony and Cleopatra*, *Coriolanus*, *Julius Caesar* and *Timon of Athens*.

227 Adolph Hitler's sketchbooks are full of architectural sketches. In a sketchbook of 1926 there is a design for a stage setting for Shakespeare's *Julius Caesar*.

228 The German architect Albert Speer, meanwhile, based the grandstand of the Zeppelinfeld on Hitler's sketch of the forum from which Brutus and Mark Antony addressed the Romans. Hitler made his Nuremburg speeches from that grandstand.

229 Orson Welles opened his Mercury Theatre Company in New York in 1937 with a production of *Julius Caesar*. The production had a strong flavour of both Nazi Germany and the Italy of Mussolini.

230 King Lear is based on a figure from British myth called King Leir, who is allegedly buried in a secret tomb underneath the River Soar.

231 In the legend, Cordelia and her husband rescue King Leir, depose Goneril and Regan and regain the throne.

232 Before Shakespeare, the story which became *King Lear* – taken from Geoffrey of Monmouth's *Historia Regum Britanniae* – appeared on the stage as a comedy.

233 King James I watched King Lear as his Christmas play in 1606.

234 In May 2014, the *Liverpool Echo* reported that staff at Liverpool's Everyman Theatre were forced to be on the alert for fainting theatregoers after they staged a production of *King Lear* with a particularly gory staging of the eye-gouging scene.

235 *Macbeth* is Shakespeare's shortest tragedy.

236 *Macbeth* is based on a real Scottish king, Mac Bethad mac Findlaích, a vassal to the Viking king Canute and cousin to the Viking Earl of Orkney Thorfinn the Mighty.

237

The witches in *Macbeth* would have delighted King James I, who wrote his own book on how to catch them: it was called *Daemonologie*. To 'consult, covenant with, entertain, employ, feed or reward a wicked or cursed spirit' or to magically cause any person to be 'destroyed, killed, wasted, consumed, pined, or lamed' became a capital offence under James I.

238

Six Danish women, a teacher and one old lady from North Berwick were later executed for trying to drown James I with witchcraft as he travelled home from Denmark to Scotland with his new wife.

239

Cymbeline, a rambling story which Samuel Johnson called absurd and imbecilic, not only relies on rings and bracelets to identify the disguised heroes and heroines but also upon the heroine's left breast, which has an unusual 'cinque-spotted' red mole on it.

240

Ben Jonson called *Pericles* – a weird story of incest, reviving corpses and pirates – a 'mouldy tale'. However, it became the first of Shakespeare's plays to be itself revived after the Restoration of Charles II and the reopening of the theatres.

241 Benedict's joke in *Much Ado*, that 'Her hair shall be of what colour it please God', refers to the Tudor love of hair dye. The *Merchant of Venice* refers to another vogue: corpse-hair wigs, 'those crisped snaky golden locks, Which make such wanton gambols with the wind … The skull that bred them in the sepulchre.'

242

Much Ado About Nothing was performed as part of the enormous celebrations for Princess Elizabeth's marriage. Elizabeth, who became known as the Winter Queen, was the Gunpowder Conspirators' choice of monarch once they'd blown up her father, James I. Instead, she became the direct ancestor of our current Queen, Elizabeth II, and indeed of most other European royal families.

243

The Taming of the Shrew was most likely written when Shakespeare first arrived in London. However, the play is difficult to date as another play, called *A Pleasant Conceited Historie, called the taming of a Shrew,* was popular at the same time!

244

If *As You Like It* hadn't been included in the First Folio it would have been lost, as it wasn't included in any of the quartos. Thomas Hardy's *Under the Greenwood Tree* takes its name from a song in this play.

245 According to Neil MacGregor, Richard II's lament that 'thoughts are minutes', for 'now hath time made me his numbering clock', was cutting-edge for Shakespeare's era: before the year 1600 most clocks counted only in hours, and had no minute hand.

246 Watches such as the one Malvolio dreams of owning were an even rarer thing. However, people could purchase a ring dial: turn the dial to the correct month, hold the ring up to the sun and a beam of light would fall on the correct hour.

247 Halliday's *Shakespeare Companion* mentions that printer Valentine Simmes introduced 69 different typos into his version of *Richard II*: the reprint corrected 14 of them, but added another 123!

248 The printing for the quarto of *Richard III*, one of Shakespeare's earliest plays, was also done by Simmes. Simmes was eventually banned from calling himself a master printer altogether.

249

Animals were frequently used in stage performances in the Elizabethan theatre. One of the stage directions in *The Winter's Tale* famously instructs: 'exit, pursued by a bear'. A real bear from the bearbaiting arena next door may have been used. In fact, many of the theatregoers at the Globe would have come from next door, having just watched a round of bear-baiting there.

250

Love's Labour's Lost contains a reference to Marocco, a famous 'dancing horse' with his own arena in London who could count, walk on two legs and was trained to bow to Queen Elizabeth. Marocco once performed on the roof of St Paul's Cathedral.

251

One of the earliest films ever made was a silent version of *King John*, made in 1899 by Victorian theatre giant and Shakespeare lover Herbert Beerbohm Tree (the grandfather of hell-raising actor Oliver Reed).

252

Like *Macbeth, All's Well that Ends Well* used to have an unlucky reputation amongst actors, after Peg Woffington, a Georgian superstar, collapsed during the first night of a revival. She never acted on stage again.

253

The Comedy of Errors was performed at Gray's Inn, home to Sir Francis Bacon, on 28 December 1594. The actors were described as 'a company of base and common fellows'.

254

In July 1914, the *Independent* reported that more than 100 members of the audience – including the paper's own reviewer – fainted or fled during the Globe's recent revival of *Titus Andronicus*.

255

Coriolanus is based on a real (or semi-mythologised) Roman general who attacked the city of Rome. His name comes from the city of Corioli, which he personally burned.

According to the Preface for the 1609 quarto of *Troilus and Cressida*, one of Shakespeare's plays would have set you back six pence when printed.

According to Paul Barry's *A Lifetime with Shakespeare*, Will Kempe's naughty dog (who starred as the original Crab in *Two Gentlemen of Verona*) was so unpopular with Shakespeare's company that they tried to have him banned from their theatre.

The printer miscalculated the space needed to include *Timon of Athens* in the First Folio, and so many of the lines were cut in half and turned into verse in order to fill up the remaining space.

Impressario Philip Henslowe, who commissioned *Two Noble Kinsmen,* lived just down the road from Shakespeare, opposite the Clink prison.

260

Shakespeare's Globe caught fire on 29 June 1613 during a performance of *Henry VIII*. The entire theatre was burnt to the ground, and had to be rebuilt the following year.

261

Sir Henry Wotton wrote a letter describing the accident at the Globe: 'The King's players had a new play, called *All is True*, representing some principal pieces of the reign of Henry VIII ... certain cannons being shot off at [Henry VIII's] entry, some of the paper or other stuff, wherewith one of them was stopped, did light on the thatch, where, being thought at first but idle smoak, and their eyes more attentive to the show, it kindled inwardly, and ran round like a train, consuming within less than an hour the whole house to the very ground...'

262

Only one theatregoer was hurt in the accident: 'One man had his breeches set on fire, that would perhaps have broyled him, if he had not, by the benefit of a provident wit, put it out with a bottle of ale.'

263

Luckily for Shakespeare,
he had already sold his stake
in the Globe before it burned.

264

*A doleful ballad of the
General Conflagration of the
famous Theatre called the
Globe* went on sale in 1613,
capitalising on this disaster.

265 Ben Jonson was most probably inside the Globe when it caught fire.

266 Many of Shakespeare's original drafts of his plays may have been lost in the fire.

267 The fire at the Globe could have had very serious consequences, as the theatre had just two narrow exits.

268 On the 5 September 1694, the town of Warwick caught fire. In the attic of the baker's, 'carelessly scatter'd and thrown about', were two large chests filled with Shakespeare's original papers and manuscripts, the baker being related to Shakespeare's family. The papers were totally destroyed.

269 The second Globe (pictured) was finally pulled down by Puritans in 1644-45.

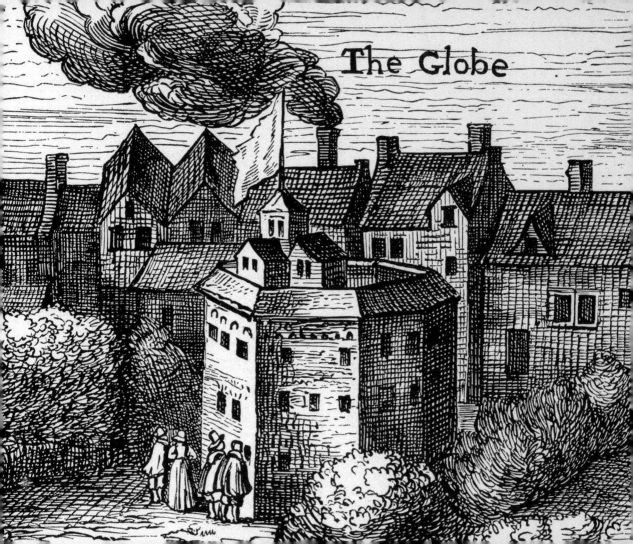
The Globe

CHAPTER THREE

Shakespeare's World

 **270** Stratford was a small but ancient hamlet in Shakespeare's time: a village has existed there from at least three centuries before the Norman Conquest.

 **271** However, the houses of most of Shakespeare's near neighbours burnt down in 1594, when Shakespeare was thirty, after a fire started in some thatch. Fire struck again the following year: more than 200 houses were lost in total, and another fifty-four houses in 1614.

 **272** Stratford was regularly visited by travelling troupes of professional actors during Shakespeare's life.

273 Weirdly, however, plays were later banned in Shakespeare's Stratford: once in December 1602, and again in February 1612.

 **274** The first known performance of a Shakespeare play in Stratford was held to fund the restoration of his memorial bust in 1746. The play was *Othello*.

275

If the family of John and Mary Shakespeare was typical of the time, young William would have had a bath once a year, in May.

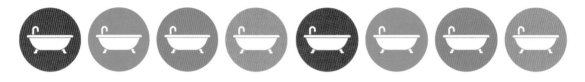

276

The annual family bath was a big occasion. The mother would fill a barrel, or the biggest tub they had. The father bathed first: then any other men who lived in the house, then the women, and finally the children, in order of their age.

277

By the time it got to the baby's turn, the water would be thick and black with all the dirt, hence the term 'don't throw the baby out with the bathwater'.

278

Shakespeare fanatic David Garrick once called Stratford 'the most dirty, unseemly, ill pav'd, wretched-looking town in all Britain'.

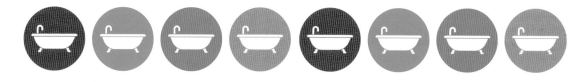

279

Elizabethans emptied their chamberpots and refuse from their windows, relying on the rain to wash the waste from dung piles, ditches, cesspits and streams into the river. There were six common dunghills in Stratford: Shakespeare's was by a hedge at the end of Henley Street.

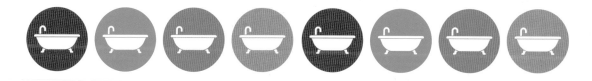

280

Stratford was quiet after sundown in Elizabethan times. According to a court judgement in 1553, no Stratford servant or apprentice was allowed out of their master's house after 'nyne by the clok', on penalty of three days in the stocks plus a stiff fine.

281

Candles were very expensive in Shakespeare's time, and so were used only for emergencies. Most writers therefore wrote in the daytime and socialised in the evenings.

282

People did not generally travel around the country during the Elizabethan age, as travelling was dangerous and expensive. Anyone who needed to travel had to get a licence from the bailiff in the Guild Hall.

283

The licence to travel ensured that the spread of disease, especially the plague, was contained. The licence also ensured that the poor and the homeless did not move from village to village. When Shakespeare moved to London he would have had to obtain just such a license.

Any stranger staying in Stratford without a licence would be put in the 'open stokes [stocks]' for three days and three nights, along with anyone who had sheltered them.

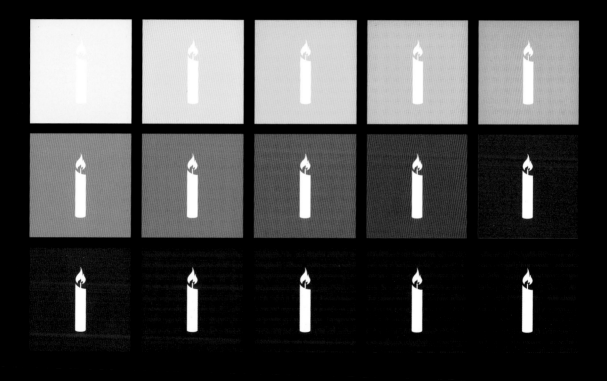

285

Most homes in Stratford did not have a proper kitchen: housewives could either cook over the hearth or take food in to a cook shop. It was illegal to bake and sell bread unless you were a licensed baker, and the price of bread was legally restricted.

286

People rose early and had a very light breakfast, such as a chunk of bread. The poor had humble and unvaried diets, consisting largely of bread, fish, cheese and ale, with vegetables if they could get them. The rich, meanwhile, added every kind of meat, including blackbirds, conger eel and peacocks.

287

Less everyday items on the menu, according to *The Good Housewifes Jewel*, included a blancmange made of sparrow brains for pudding.

288

Until 1585, eating fish was actually a legal requirement on certain days unless you bought a 'flesh-eating licence', in order to help the livelihoods of the fishermen (known as 'trinkermen').

289

However, chicken was helpfully categorised as a fish in Shakespeare's time.

290

Southwark, home to the Globe, was London's entertainment zone. The theatres, surrounded by inns, taverns, cockpits, gambling houses and brothels, were here, outside of the City's limits.

291

The Southwark inns and taverns sold cheap ale, which people generally drank instead of water. However, water was available at your house if you paid for a water carrier to bring it to you – or, in wealthier households, through plumbed-in pipes.

292

Jehan Scheyfve, ambassador to the Holy Roman Empire from May 1550 to October 1553, reported that the English were 'wont to live in pleasure-seeking and intemperance, haunt taverns and become wholly idle and disorderly'.

293

Jacobean writer Philip Stubbs (or Stubbes) claimed that England 'was so fraught with maltworms [drinkers], night and day that you would wonder to see them'.

294

Iago in *Othello* describes England as 'most potent in potting': 'your Dane, your German, and your swag-bellied Hollander, – Drink, ho! – are nothing to your English ... he drinks you, with facility, your Dane dead drunk ... he gives your Hollander a vomit, ere the next pottle can be filled.'

295

Black was a very expensive dye in Shakespeare's time. Other colours and fabrics (such as blue velvet) were actually illegal for common folk to wear under Elizabeth I's sumptuary laws against extravagance by the lower ranks.

296

Women in Shakespeare's world wore 'corked' shoes: high heels. One contemporary verse went 'these corked shoes to beare them hie ... They mince it with a pace so strange, Like untam'd heifers, when they range.'

297

Hamlet mentions the player's high heels in Act 2: 'Your Ladyship is nearer to heaven, than when I saw you last, by the altitude of a chopine [a Venetian stilt shoe which could be up to a foot high].'

298

Men wore mirrored broaches and ornaments on their hats, and women on their belts and fans, so they could check how they looked.

299

William Harrison complained that Elizabethan clothing, with its 'fardingels' and 'diversely coloured nether stocks' (stockings), meant that 'women are become men; and the men transformed into monsters'.

300

Some early Elizabethan men (and again in James I's reign) wore Venetian breeches: shorts stuffed with hair, wool and rags so that they swelled up to a massive size. The *Pedigree of the English Gallant* mentions a man who removed, in court, 'a pair of sheets, two table cloths, ten napkins, four shirts, a brush, a glass, a comb, night-caps, &c.' from inside his breeches.

301

Elizabeth I issued more royal orders about clothes than any other English ruler in history. From 1571 to 1597, for example, to help boost the wool trade, every common person above the age of six was ordered to wear a wool cap on Sundays and holidays.

302

Elizabeth herself wore furs, including lynx skins, given to her by Ivan the Terrible.

303

Shakespearean-era fashions for men varied wildly, but in one popular look Jacobean men wore their hair to their shoulders, sometimes with a 'love-lock' curling under the left ear. They added tall hats (sometimes made of beaver) rising 'like the speare or the shaft of a steeple'. Sometimes the hats were embroidered with gold and had a hat-band studded with gems, with feathers (or a lover's glove) tucked into the band.

304

Beards were dyed: red was one fashionable colour, but Bottom in *Midsummer's Night Dream* mentions a beard that was 'purple-in-grain'.

305

Shakespeare wore a gold earring in his left ear. (Earrings were common in the upper and middle ranks.)

306

THE HIGHE AND MIGHTIE PRINCE, Iames THE SEXT BY THE GRACE OF GOD KINGE OF SCOTLANDE. R.E. *fint*.

Women often wore masks in the street, to ward off sun and dust, so that (as Stubbs put it) a man 'would think he met a monster or a Devul, for face he can shew none, but two broad holes against their eyes, with glasses in them'. The other option was mufflers: strips of linen bandage worn across the lower face.

307

Weapons were common in Shakespeare's time. Shakespeare probably wore a sword; he left one to Thomas Combe in his will. The fashion for carrying knives and wearing long blades eventually led to a ban on swords longer than a yard (just under a metre): guards were appointed to snap your sword at the city gates if you exceeded this.

308

In Shakespearean Stratford it was illegal for a craftsmen or an apprentice to carry 'sword, dager, or other weypone' in the town. If you did, the local officer (Shakespeare's father, in some years) could take it from you – and if you resisted that, you were 'ponyshed' [punished] with a day and a night in the stocks.

309

Henry VIII and his children banned all labourers under the age of forty from playing football, tennis, bowls, and dice games on Sundays and holy days: they were supposed to practice their archery instead. In Stratford, locals had been fined for organising 'onlauffull bowlynge' amongst the local servants and workers.

310

Every man under sixty had to keep a longbow in his house and practice with it. However, a new weapon was in vogue: 'handegunnes'. Guns grew so common that, in 1568, one unfortunate Londoner who fired into the air in celebration accidentally shot one of the queen's men as he rowed her down the Thames.

311

When commuting between Stratford and London, Shakespeare stayed at the Crown Inn in Oxford.

312

The landlord of the Crown was John Davenant. John's son, William, grew up to be Poet Laureate, playwright and actor; Sir William Davenant (as he became) used to boast that he was the natural son of Shakespeare. Sir William later adapted many of Shakespeare's plays with his own company, The Duke of York's Men, including *Hamlet*, *Julius Caesar* and *The Tempest*.

313

Sir William also had personal experience of one of Shakespearean England's perils: he lost his nose to syphilis in his twenties. Diseases such as plague, pox, tuberculosis and 'agues' reduced the average lifespan of a Tudor working man to twenty-five, and a wealthier man to thirty-five.

314

Liza Picard's fantastic *Elizabeth's London* includes some amazing Tudor remedies, including taking 'the lungs of a fox washed in wine, herbs and liquorice' for asthma, or 'a whole unicorn horn' to treat a case of poisoning.

315 There was an earthquake in London in 1580.

316 When Shakespeare arrived in London, the star playwright was the brilliant young Christopher Marlowe. Shakespeare may have started his writing career by collaborating on a play with him. Marlowe led a dangerous double life, with involvement in espionage: he was murdered in a Deptford pub in 1593.

317 London Bridge was the only bridge that connected the northern and southern sides of Elizabethan London. Shakespeare would have walked across it several times a week.

318

Well-off Elizabethan commuters hired ferrymen to ferry them across and along the Thames instead of taking the bridge. The Thames was thus usually crowded with rowing boats, barges, and commercial sailing ships.

319

As Shakespeare crossed London Bridge, the impaled heads of executed traitors would have looked down on him, reminding him to be careful about becoming involved in politics. As a further warning, sections of quartered criminals were also hung from the city's gates.

320

Shakespeare would have done his shopping on London Bridge, using the many shops built on the structure. Some of the buildings there were four storeys high, houses for prosperous merchants as well as shop fronts.

321

Shakespeare would almost certainly have visited the Royal Exchange on Threadneedle Street, opened by the queen in 1571. It was the world's first shopping mall, a huge arcaded building with banking facilities and accommodation for 150 shops. The building surrounded a courtyard where 4,000 bankers and tradesmen conducted their business.

322

As in a modern shopping mall, the Royal Exchange offered everything the people of the time could have wished for, and it made London Europe's top shopping destination. One could buy wigs, jewellery, perfume, hats, shoes, breeches, shirts, ruffles, feathers, silks, drugs, wine, spices, paper, ink, candles, toys, and anything else you could think of there.

323

One of the most lucrative products offered by merchants was starch, and starchers conducted a brisk trade. Portraits of Elizabethans show some splendid ruffs, intricately made and expensively starched. There was even a brief fashion for wearing three ruffs at once.

ELISABET D. G. ANGLIÆ, FRANCIÆ, ET HIBERNIÆ REGINA, FID. CHR. PROP.

Mortua Anno Miseri Cordiæ, Æt 70

324

Whitehall Palace – the largest palace in Europe, with over 1,500 rooms – had a cock-fighting pit (as well as a bowling green, an indoor tennis court and a jousting tiltyard).

325

One could see dogfights and cockfights in Southwark, but bear baiting was the favourite sport of the era. The Swiss physician, traveller and diarist Thomas Platter attended a performance of *Julius Caesar* at the Globe theatre in 1599 and was offended by a stench that pervaded the theatre. After the performance, he went round the back and found 120 English mastiffs, twelve bears and several bulls, all baited in the arena next door.

326

Platter entered in his diary: 'The place [the Globe] was evil-smelling because of the lights [offal] and meat on which the butchers fed the said dogs.'

327

The Globe was the only London theatre dedicated solely to plays: animals fought at all the others between performances. Queen Elizabeth I even dedicated a whole day (Thursday) to 'bear baiting and such pastimes', and plays were banned on that day.

328

In July 1596 Shakespeare and his Southwark neighbours may have made an official complaint about the nuisances caused by Alleyn's Bear Gardens. (In the same year, a man called William Wayte complained that *he* had been assaulted outside the Swan Theatre by a gang including one William Shakespeare.)

329

There was a disaster at the Bear Garden in 1583: the scaffolding, crowded with people, suddenly fell, and eight people were killed and many more severely wounded.

330 Tudor women did not wear knickers.

331 In general, Tudor and Stuart women married a lot later than Juliet (who is fourteen): in their twenties, and even late twenties.

332 Illegitimacy was relatively rare, but nonetheless Shakespearean England experienced some truly bizarre sex scandals. David Cressy's *Travesties and Transgressions*, for example, explores the case of Agnes Bowker who, in 1569, gave birth to a cat. (The investigator's notes ended up in the hands of William Cecil, Queen Elizabeth I's Secretary of State.)

333 Tudor methods of contraception included inserting bundles of herbs like nettles and parsley, wool soaked with chemicals like vinegar or even, according to some scholars, inserting lumps of wood or stones to hinder conception.

334

Just down the road from the Globe, in Paris Gardens, was Holland's Leaguer, a huge fortified brothel (with its own moat and drawbridge) run by 'Bess' Holland. Prostitutes were known as 'queans', and Bess Holland's finest charged £20 just for dinner.

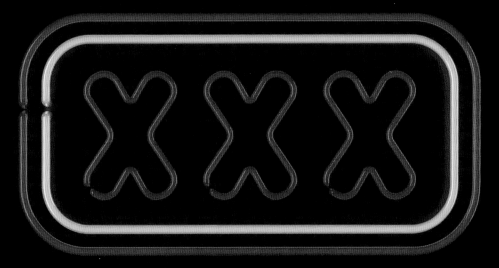

335

Bankside waitresses who were willing to offer you a little extra with your drink wore white aprons to distinguish them from their non-wanton colleagues.

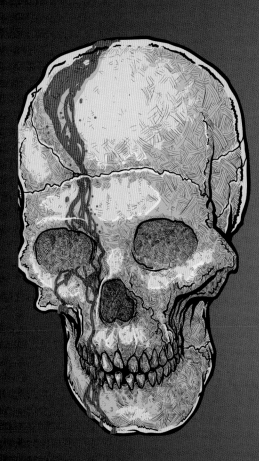

336

Apart from bear baiting and the theatre, public executions were Elizabethan Londoners' most popular spectator activity. Londoners could go to Tower Hill, where the upper-class condemned were beheaded; they could see hangings of common criminals at Tyburn or Smithfield; more rarely, they could also see drawing and quarterings of traitors.

337

Playwriting was a dangerous business in Elizabethan times: Ben Jonson was twice imprisoned for writing political satires, for instance.

338

Jonson's thumb was also branded with a *T* – for Tyburn, London's place of execution – after killing an actor in a duel. He only escaped execution for the crime by reading the 'neck verse', Psalm 51: ' Have mercy on me, O God, according to your unfailing love.'

339

It was a crime in Shakespeare's lifetime to whistle in the City of London after nine o'clock at night: the penalty was imprisonment.

340

Church attendance was compulsory in Shakespeare's time, and non-attendance was also a crime: Shakespeare would have attended twice every Sunday for as long as he lived, on pain of a fine.

341

Shakespeare's plays repeat some of the wild stories told by Shakespearean mariners returning from the voyages of discovery in the new worlds. For example, Othello says he has seen 'the Anthrophopagi, and men whose heads / Do grow beneath their shoulders'.

342

Shakespeare's world included North African influences. Queen Elizabeth I even had a 'Moorish' title, given to her by the King of Morocco: 'the Sultana Isabel'.

343

Sir Francis Drake sailed around the entire world in Shakespeare's lifetime, returning in 1580, when Shakespeare was sixteen, with so much captured treasure that he doubled England's income for the year.

344

Walter Raleigh, famous for bringing American tobacco and potatoes to England, never actually visited North America – only South America. His entire North American colony vanished from Roanoke Island in North Carolina in one of the greatest mysteries of the age, leaving only a mysterious message (CROATOAN) carved into a tree.

345

The very first museum in Britain, a 'cabinet of curiosities', opened in London in Shakespeare's time. John Tradescante's Musaeum Tradescantianum contained everything from 'ftrange Fifhes' and hummingbirds to penguins, dodos, a hippopotamus, an 'Alegator from Egypt', a lion's head, an elephant's tail, a 'sharke', and a banana.

346

Discovery turned inward as well as outward in Tudor times: Henry VIII legalised dissection, so Shakespeare lived in a world that had access to all 273 of Vesalius' detailed illustrations of the inside of the human body (plus the real thing too, if so desired).

CHAPTER FOUR

Shakespearean Trivia

347 When the Revd Thomas Bowdler published his ten-volume *Family Shakespeare* in 1818, he cut any passage that, in his opinion, hinted at obscenity (including Hamlet's conversations with Ophelia). The verb 'to bowdlerise' is today used to describe crass and insensitive censoring.

348 *Hamlet* is the most frequently performed and adapted play around the world: it has been calculated that a performance of *Hamlet* begins somewhere in the world every minute of every day.

349 Agatha Christie's play *The Mousetrap* takes its title from the play within the play in *Hamlet*. It opened at the St Martin's Theatre in March 1978 and is still on today, the longest-running play in London's West End.

350 'I don't make much distinction,' Ian McKellen once said, 'between being a stand-up comic and acting Shakespeare – in fact, unless you're a good comedian, you're never going to be able to play Hamlet properly.'

351 The best quote on Hamlet, however, has to come from Oscar Wilde: 'Are the commentators on *Hamlet* really mad,' he wrote, 'or only pretending to be?'

352 William Shakespeare's name has some amusing anagrams, including 'We shall make a pie, sir!', 'Hear me, as I will speak' and 'I swear I'll make heaps'.

353 Perhaps the most amusing anagram for 'William Shakespeare', however, is 'I am a weakish speller'.

354 'William Shakespeare, the Bard of Avon' is an anagram of 'abrasive alpha male of the worse kind.'

355 'The Immortal Bard, William Shakespeare' is an anagram of 'this admirable writer shall make a poem'.

356 Bates' *The Darling Buds of May*, Proust's *Remembrance of Things Past*, William Faulkner's *The Sound and the Fury*, Aldous Huxley's *Brave New World* and Truman Capote's *In Cold Blood* all take their titles from Shakespeare.

357

'Bard' is a Scottish word, and was originally applied to the poet Robert Burns. It means 'local poet': that's why Shakespeare is known as 'the Bard of Avon'.

358

(a shoemaker) living in Stratford at the same time as Shakespeare's father. There may also have been another (unrelated) Anne Hathaway living in Shottery in 1580.

359

Stratford's town hall was blown up during the English Civil Wars, when five barrels of gunpowder were either accidentally – or deliberately – set off, killing one Stratford man and wounding another five.

360

In 1810, William Shakespeare's seal ring was found by a woman working in a field near the church at Stratford. In a weird coincidence, one of the men working nearby was called William Shakespeare.

361

In the 1860s, a death mask which may – or may not – have been taken from the last remains of William Shakespeare himself was found in a junk shop and sold at auction in Germany. Dr Hammerschmidt-Hummel published a paper in *New Scientist* in 1995 arguing that this mask suggests that Shakespeare died of eye cancer.

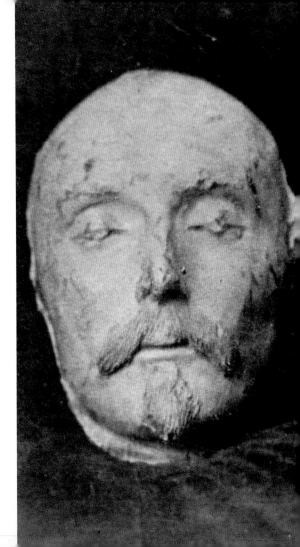

362 Bill Bryson counts '138,198 commas, 26,794 colons, and 15,785 question marks' in Shakespeare's works.

363 According to Bryson, eccentric Shakespeare researcher Charles Wallace eventually came to believe that 'the British government was secretly employing large numbers of students to uncover Shakespeare records before he could get to them'.

364 The twenty-seven most recently discovered moons of Uranus were named by the International Astronomy Union after characters created by Shakespeare and Alexander Pope.

365 L.G. Bowell discovered 550 asteroids between Mars and Jupiter. He named a very small one, discovered in 1983, '2985 Shakespeare'.

366

In a 1963 debate in Oxford, Malcolm X quoted the first few lines of 'to be or not to be' - incidentally the most quoted line of poetry in all literature in the English language, and also the most searched-for Shakespeare quote on the internet - to make a point about 'extremism in defence of liberty'.

367 The only Chinese literary journal devoted to a non-Chinese man of letters is *Shakespeare Studies*, published by the *Shakespeare Society of China*.

368 There is no 'Shakespeare Tavern' in Stratford, and only three pubs in London carry that name. There is one very interesting 'Shakespeare Tavern' which, alas, doesn't exist anywhere but in the history books about New York: it's Thomas Hodgkinson's Shakespeare Tavern, which opened in 1808 on the corner of Nassau and Fulton streets.

369 Famous drinkers at the Shakespeare Tavern, New York, included 'the Lads of Kilkenny', a group of young writers, actors and politicians: prosperous, professional young men interested in literature whose leader was Washington Irving, author of Rip Van Winkle.

370

In September 2015, the Stratford-upon-Avon Herald revealed that the Royal Shakespeare Company sold more than 1.8 million tickets during the 2014/2015 season, staging 28 productions and co-productions and putting on 2,048 performances.

371

Shakespeare often mentioned the flowers of his native Warwickshire in his plays. He was particularly fond of its violets: 'Like the sweet sound that breathes upon a bank of violets' and 'From her fair and unpolluted flesh may violets spring!' are just a few examples.

372

D.H. Lawrence once said: 'When I read Shakespeare, I am struck with wonder that such trivial people should muse and thunder in such lovely language.'

373

Dickens also performed Shakespeare's plays in amateur productions, and was a member of both the Shakespeare Club and the Shakespeare Society.

374

Charles Dickens' work is drenched in Shakespeare. As one of Shakespeare's most ardent admirers, his work contains more than 1,000 references to (and quotations from) the Bard. He was deeply involved in the purchase of the Birthplace as a place of pilgrimage.

375

Dame Ellen Terry, meanwhile, was delighted by what she saw as Shakespeare's Feminism: 'Wonderful women! Have you ever thought how much we all, and women especially, owe to Shakespeare for his vindication of women in these fearless, high-spirited, resolute and intelligent heroines?'

 **376** Shakespeare's plays are still performed more than those of any other playwright, living or dead, and have been translated into every major language.

 **377** Julius Nyerere, then president of Tanzania, translated *Julius Caesar* and *The Merchant of Venice* into Swahili.

378 Two of Shakespeare's plays, *Hamlet* and *Much Ado About Nothing*, have even been translated into Klingon. The Klingon Language Institute plans to translate more.

 **379** Shakespeare's sonnets and seventeen of his plays have been translated into Esperanto. The first was *Hamleto* in 1894.

380

More than 600 films give Shakespeare a writing credit, and about 300 are based on *Hamlet*, *Romeo and Juliet*, *Macbeth* or *Othello*. Disney's *The Lion King*, for example, is based on *Hamlet*.

381

Some extremely surprising film stars have performed in film adaptations of *Hamlet*, including William Shatner and Arnold Schwarzenegger.

382

Shatner later said: 'Shakespeare's words are a little strange, but ... you will recognise the situation he deals with: death, life, honour, respect... If it's well spoken, if the actors know what they're doing, you'll get the meaning, and the meaning has universality.'

383

A science-fiction film, *Forbidden Planet*, set on a lonely planet, is actually the story of *The Tempest*.

384

Star Trek, meanwhile, took many of its episode titles from Shakespeare, including: *How Sharper than a Serpent's Tooth* (*King Lear*); *Sins of the Father* (*The Merchant of Venice*); *The Dagger of the Mind* (*Macbeth*); *All our Yesterdays* (*Macbeth*); *Wink of an Eye* (*A Midsummer Night's Dream*); *By Any Other Name* (*Romeo and Juliet*); *The Conscience of the King* (*Hamlet*); *Heart of Stone* (*Othello*); *Once More Unto the Breach* (*Henry V*); *The Dogs of War* (*Julius Caesar*); *Mortal Coil* (*Hamlet*).

385

There is a thirteenth-century house in Verona where Shakespeare's Juliet is said to have lived.

386

The house, the *Casa di Giulietta*, once belonged to the Capello family and is one of Verona's main tourist attractions. The combination of the similar name to Capulet and the fact that it has a balcony that looks out over a courtyard has turned it into 'Juliet's balcony' – the 'real' balcony where Romeo courted Juliet.

387

Suicide occurs an
unlucky thirteen times
in Shakespeare's plays,
including in *Romeo and
Juliet* and *Julius Caesar*.

388

In 1751 the London Company of Comedians, under the direction of Lewis Hallam, landed in Virginia, where the ban on the immigration of actors had recently been lifted. Their first production was *The Merchant of Venice*, which played to mixed groups of settlers and Native Americans.

389

The first American performance of *Hamlet* was also by Lewis Hallam, who played the lead role in their production of the play in Philadelphia in 1759.

390

There were theatre companies established in America as early as 1810. Charles Kean, the great Shakespearean actor, began a tour in 1831 in New York: in total, the tour took him an astonishing fifteen years.

391

During his presidency George Washington encouraged theatre-going. Despite the continuing animosity towards anything British, citizens of the new nation continued to love Shakespeare (who became equally fashionable on both sides of the Atlantic).

392

John Adams and his son John Quincy Adams were avid Shakespeare readers.

393

American President Abraham Lincoln was a lover of Shakespeare's plays and frequently quoted from them to his friends; he also used them liberally in his speeches.

394

Famous American Shakespearean actor Junius Brutus Booth took his *Hamlet* to San Francisco in 1851. John Wilkes Booth, Junius' son, was also an extremely popular Shakespearean actor. He is best known, however, for assassinating the President of the United States. Edwin Booth, John's older brother, played the role of Hamlet for 100 nights at the Winter Garden Theatre, New York, in the 1864/65 season.

395

John Harvard, benefactor of Harvard College in the United States, was married to Katherine Rogers of Stratford-upon-Avon. The Harvard house in Stratford is still popular with American tourists today.

396

The US has Shakespeare to thank for its estimated 200 million starlings. In 1890 an American Bardolator, Eugene Schieffelin, embarked on a project to import each species of bird mentioned in Shakespeare's works. Part of this project involved releasing two flocks of sixty starlings in New York's Central Park.

397 The famous film magnate Samuel Goldwyn gave this review of Shakespeare's plays: 'Fantastic! And it was all written with a feather!'

398 Bill Clinton, influenced by memorizing a long passage in high school, once said, 'Mr Shakespeare made me a better President.'

399 There are more pages referring to Shakespeare (160 million) on Google than for God (140 million) and Elvis Presley (2.7 million) combined.

400 Shakespeare is beaten only by the 200 million Google results for Barack Obama. During the next 400 years, however, he will no doubt overtake the President.

Short Bibliography

Modern

1599: A Year in the Life of Shakespeare by James Shapiro
Elizabeth's London by Liza Picard
The 'Penguin Classics' editions of Shakespeare's plays (various)
The Time-Traveller's Guide to Elizabethan England by Ian Mortimer
Shakespeare's Britain by Jonathan Bate and Dora Thornton with Becky Allen
Shakespeare's Restless World: An Unexpected History in Twenty Objects by Neil MacGregor

Shakespeare: The World as a Stage by Bill Bryson
The Shakespeare Thefts: In Search of the First Folios by Eric Rasmussen
Shakespeare's Local by Pete Brown
Shakespeare Beyond Doubt: Evidence, Argument, Controversy edited by Paul Edmondson and Stanley Wells
Travesties and Transgressions in Tudor and Stuart England: Tales of Discord by David Cress

Antiquarian

Stratford upon Avon: the Home of William Shakespeare Delineated
A Guide to Stratford upon Avon by R.B. Wheler
Shakespeare and Stratford Upon Avon: A Chronicle of the Time by Robert E. Hunter
The Life of William Shakespeare Including Many Particulars Respecting the Poet and His Family Never Before Published by James Orchard Halliwell
The Stratford Shakespeare by Charles Knight

Old and New London
Sumptuary Legislation and Personal Regulation In England by Frances Elisabeth Baldwin (dissertation, 1923)
Shakespeare and His Times: Including the Biography of the Poet by Nathan Drake
Extracts from the Accounts of the Revels at Court, Volume 13, Issue 1 by Peter Cunningham

Websites

www.findingshakespeare.co.uk
www.nosweatshakespeare.com

http://shalt.dmu.ac.uk
http://www.shakespearesengland.co.uk

Picture Credits